First Facts®

Water All Around

The Water Cycle

by Rebecca Olien

Consultant:
Peter R. Jaffé, Professor
Department of Civil and Environmental Engineering
Princeton University
Princeton, New Jersey

Capstone press®
Mankato, Minnesota

D1293735

First Facts is published by Capstone Press,
151 Good Counsel Drive, P.O. Box 669, Mankato, Minnesota 56002.
www.capstonepub.com

Library of Congress Cataloging-in-Publication Data
Olien, Rebecca.
    The water cycle / by Rebecca Olien.
    p. cm.—(First facts. Water all around)
    Includes bibliographical references and index.
    ISBN-13: 978-0-7368-3701-9 (hardcover)
    ISBN-10: 0-7368-3701-9 (hardcover)
    ISBN-13: 978-0-7368-5182-8 (softcover pbk.)
    ISBN-10: 0-7368-5182-4 (softcover pbk.)
    1. Water cycle—Juvenile literature. I. Title. II. Series.
GB848.O58 2005
551.48—dc22   2004010896

Summary: Explains the stages of the water cycle and how the water cycle impacts the earth's
    water supply.

Editorial Credits
Christine Peterson, editor; Linda Clavel, designer; Ted Williams, illustrator; Kelly Garvin,
    photo researcher; Scott Thoms, photo editor

Photo Credits
Brand X Pictures, cover
Bruce Coleman Inc./Bruce Clendenning, 14; Jane Burton, 17
Copyright 2004, Christopher Srnka, all rights reserved, 20
Corbis/Dex Images Inc., 10–11; Ed Bock, 16; Roy Morsch, 9
David R. Frazier Photolibrary, 8
Index Stock Imagery/Omni Photo Communications Inc., 12–13
Photodisc/StockTrek, 4–5
Tom Stack & Associates Inc./Thomas Kitchin, 18–19
Transparencies Inc./Jane Faircloth, 15

Table of Contents

Water Covers the Earth 4

The Water Cycle 6

Evaporation 8

Humidity 10

Condensation 13

Clouds 14

Precipitation 16

An Endless Cycle 19

Amazing but True! 20

Hands On: Water Cycle Cups 21

Glossary 22

Read More 23

Internet Sites 23

Index 24

Water Covers the Earth

When seen from space, the earth is a swirl of blue oceans and white clouds. Water covers 70 percent of the earth. Clouds form when water rises into the air as **vapor**. Water falls as rain or snow. Water moves and changes as part of the water **cycle**.

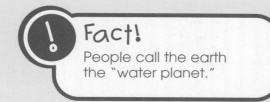

Fact!
People call the earth the "water planet."

4

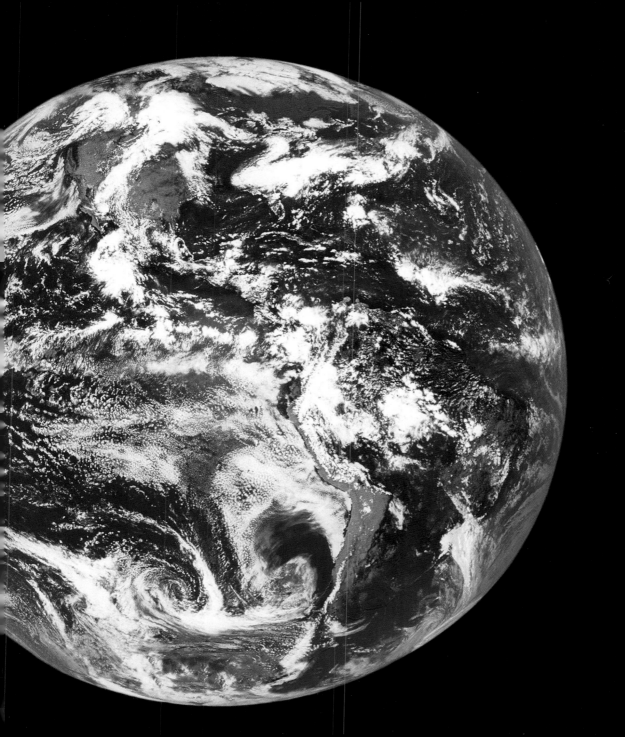

The Water Cycle

Water changes as it moves through the water cycle. Water **evaporates** as it changes from a **liquid** into a gas. Water vapor **condenses** to form clouds. **Precipitation** falls from clouds as rain and snow. The sun's heat turns liquid water back into vapor. The water cycle begins again.

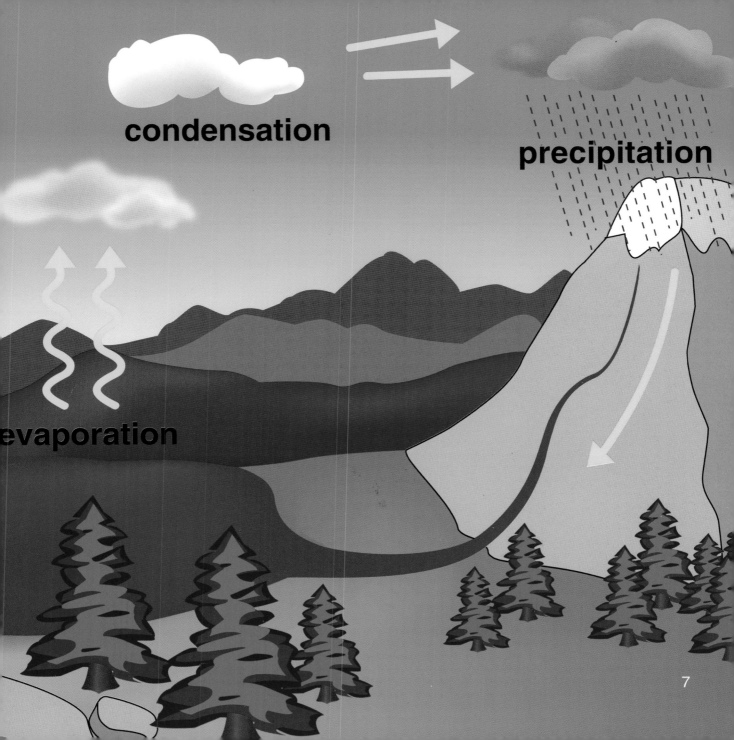

condensation

precipitation

evaporation

7

Evaporation

Water evaporates when it changes from a liquid to a gas. The sun's heat makes water evaporate.

People can't see water vapor. Vapor can only be seen when it is mixed with water drops. We can see vapor as steam when water boils.

Humidity

Humidity is the amount of water vapor in the air. Humidity changes with the temperature. Warm air holds more water vapor than cold air. People feel warmer on humid days because sweat does not evaporate quickly.

Fun Fact!
Your hair is longer on humid days. Water vapor makes hair heavier.

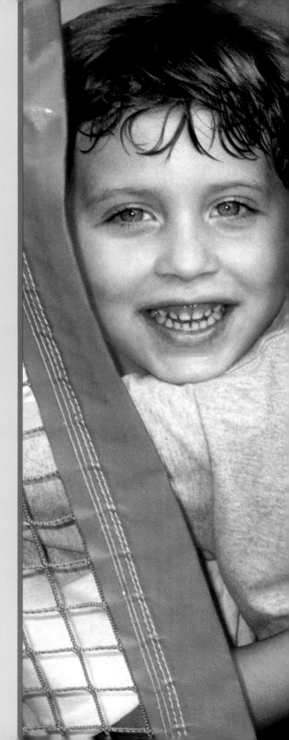

Condensation

Condensation takes place when water changes from a gas into a liquid. Vapor turns into drops as air cools. We can see condensation as dew drops on leaves. Condensation drops also slide down a glass of ice water.

Fun Fact!
Raindrops are not shaped like tears. Raindrops are balls that get wider as they fall.

Clouds

Clouds form when water vapor condenses. Water vapor condenses onto specks of dust. These drops stick together to make clouds.

Clouds grow heavy with water as condensation takes place. Dark clouds are filled with water. Rain is on the way.

Precipitation

Water falls from clouds as precipitation. Rain falls when clouds fill with water. Frozen water falls as snow, sleet, or hail.

Precipitation **recharges** water on the earth. Rain **seeps** into the soil to restore water in the ground. It flows over land. It fills rivers, lakes, and oceans.

An Endless Cycle

Water always flows and changes. Water from oceans, lakes, and rivers evaporates under the sun. Drops of water vapor stick together to make clouds. Water returns to the earth as rain and snow. The water cycle never ends.

Fun Fact!
Scientists have names for 26 different types of clouds.

Amazing but True!

The water people drink today is the same water dinosaurs drank millions of years ago. The earth's water is about 3 billion years old. The water cycle keeps water on the planet. In the years to come, people, plants, and animals will also use this same water.

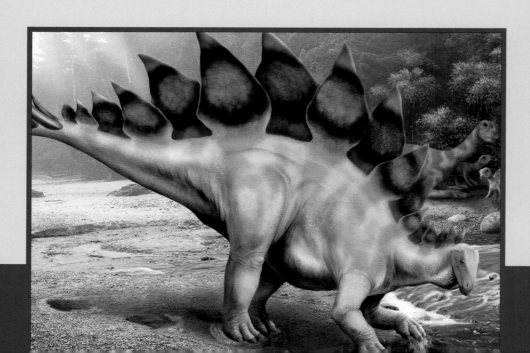

Hands On: Water Cycle Cups

Water is the only substance found in nature as a liquid, a solid, and a gas. Try this activity to see how water changes into its different forms as part of the water cycle.

What You Need

2 clear plastic cups
hot tap water
ice cube

What You Do

1. Fill one plastic cup with about 1 inch (2.5 centimeters) of hot tap water.
2. Quickly place the second cup upside down on top of the first cup. Make sure that the rims of the cups are connected.
3. Place an ice cube on top of the stacked cups.
4. Look for the different states of water in the water cycle. Water vapor rises into the top cup. The ice cools the air so tiny droplets form. As the drops get bigger, they fall back into the cup like rain.

Glossary

condense (kuhn-DENSS)—to change from a gas into a liquid

cycle (SYE-kuhl)—something that happens over and over again

evaporate (e-VAP-uh-rate)—the action of a liquid changing into vapor or a gas

humidity (hyoo-MIH-du-tee)—the measure of the moisture in the air

liquid (LIK-wid)—a substance that flows freely

precipitation (pri-sip-i-TAY-shuhn)—water that falls from the sky as rain, sleet, snow, or hail

recharge (ri-CHARJ)—to bring back to an original state

seep (SEEP)—to flow or trickle slowly

vapor (VAY-pur)—a substance in gas form

Read More

Pringle, Laurence P. *Come to the Ocean's Edge: A Nature Cycle Book.* Honesdale, Pa.: Boyds Mills Press, 2003.

Sherman, Josepha. *Shapes in the Sky: A Book About Clouds.* Amazing Science. Minneapolis: Picture Window Books, 2004.

Waldman, Neil. *The Snowflake: A Water Cycle Story.* Brookfield, Conn.: Millbrook Press, 2003.

Internet Sites

FactHound offers a safe, fun way to find Internet sites related to this book. All of the sites on FactHound have been researched by our staff.

Here's how:
1. Visit *www.facthound.com*
2. Type in this special code **0736837019** for age-appropriate sites. Or enter a search word related to this book for a more general search.
3. Click on the **Fetch It** button.

FactHound will fetch the best sites for you!

Index

clouds, 4, 6, 14–15, 16, 19
condensation, 6, 13, 14, 15

dinosaurs, 20

earth, 4, 17, 19, 20
evaporation, 6, 8, 10, 19

gas, 6, 8, 13

hail, 16
humidity, 10

lakes, 17, 19
liquids, 6, 8, 13

oceans, 4, 17, 19

precipitation, 6, 16–17

rain, 4, 6, 13, 15, 16, 17, 19
rivers, 17, 19

sleet, 16
snow, 4, 6, 16, 19

temperature, 10

vapor, 4, 6, 9, 10, 13, 14, 19

water drops, 9, 13, 14, 19